THE HISTORY OF THE
NEW YORK
YANKEES

MICHAEL E. GOODMAN

CREATIVE 🍎 EDUCATION

Published by Creative Education, 123 South Broad Street, Mankato, MN 56001

Creative Education is an imprint of The Creative Company.

Designed by Rita Marshall.

Photographs by Associated Press/Wide World Photos, Icon Sports Media (David N. Seelig),

Sports Gallery (John Sandhaus, Al Messerschmidt), SportsChrome (Rob Tringali Jr., Michael Zito),

TimePix (John G. Zimmerman)

Library of Congress Cataloging-in-Publication Data

Goodman, Michael E. The history of the New York Yankees / by Michael Goodman.

p. cm. — (Baseball)   ISBN 1-58341-217-4

Summary: A team history of the organization that has won twenty-two World Series

titles and thirty-four American League pennants.

1. New York Yankees (Baseball team)—History—

Juvenile literature. [1. New York Yankees (Baseball team)—History.

2. Baseball—History.] I. Title. II. Baseball (Mankato, Minn.).

GV875.N4 G66 2002   796.357'64'097471—dc21   2001047865

First Edition 9 8 7 6 5 4 3 2 1

ALTHOUGH

IT IS LOCATED IN A SMALL CORNER OF THE NORTH-

eastern part of the United States, the city of New York is at the

center of the country's business, cultural, and artistic life. New York

seems to have more of everything than any other city in the United

States—more people, businesses, buildings, restaurants, cars, lights,

and action. A popular song claims, "If I can make it there, I'll make it

anywhere." And every year, thousands of people from all over the

world come to New York to try to make their mark there.

One group that has certainly made it in New York is the city's

American League (AL) baseball team, the New York Yankees.

The Yankees are the most successful sports franchise in American

history, boasting more championships, more records, and more

MILLER HUGGINS

superstars than any other team in sports. The team got off to a slow

start, but since then, it has set an unmatched standard of excellence.

{RUTH AND GEHRIG LEAD THE WAY} When

the club began play in 1903, it wasn't the best team in

the AL or even in New York; both the New York Giants

and Brooklyn Dodgers of the National League (NL)

were more successful franchises. The Yankees came

close to a pennant in 1904 and then settled into the bottom half of

the league standings for the next 15 years.

Finally, in 1918, a feisty manager named Miller Huggins took

control of the Yankees. Huggins built his team around power hit-

ting, and his 1919 club led the AL with 45 home runs. That same

year, outfielder Babe Ruth of the Boston Red Sox hit 29 homers all

by himself, and Huggins convinced Yankees owner Jacob Ruppert to

obtain Ruth for New York. When Ruth hit 54 home runs for the

REGGIE JACKSON

1920 Yankees, he not only set new club and league records, he also

out-homered almost every other *team* in baseball.

Ruth helped turn the Yankees into big winners, but he didn't do the job alone. In 1923, star first baseman Lou Gehrig joined the club, and the duo became the key components of a slugging lineup known as "Murderers' Row." Behind Ruth and Gehrig, the Yankees won five AL pennants and four World Series titles between 1923 and 1932. In all, Ruth played on seven Yankees pennant winners, while Gehrig contributed to nine pennants and eight world championships.

Second baseman Tony Lazzeri was a key part of the powerful "Murderers' Row" lineup.

Ruth and Gehrig had very different personalities and styles. Ruth was playful and outgoing, a little boy in a man's body; Gehrig was serious and reserved. Ruth was perhaps the most loved person in America in the 1920s, especially by kids and his teammates. Said Yankees pitcher Waite Hoyt, "To play on the same club with Ruth

9

TONY LAZZERI

Built in **1920**, Yankee Stadium has become perhaps the game's most famous ballpark.

YANKEE STADIUM

was not only a pleasure, it was a privilege. . . . Babe was no ordinary man. He was superman to the ballplayers." Before retiring in 1935,

In **1929**, the Yankees became the first team to permanently add numbers to their uniforms.

Ruth compiled a lifetime batting average of .342 and hit 714 home runs, still the second-highest total in major-league history.

While Ruth was known for towering, tape-measure blasts, Gehrig was more of a line-drive hitter. "He could hit a ball harder in every direction than any man who ever played," said Yankees catcher Bill Dickey. Gehrig's lifetime totals are nearly as remarkable as Ruth's: a .342 average, 493 homers, and 1,995 RBI. But most impressive of all was his durability. Between 1925 and 1939, Gehrig played in 2,130 consecutive games (a record that lasted until Baltimore Orioles shortstop Cal Ripken Jr. surpassed it in 1995). What finally stopped his streak was an incurable muscle disease called amyotrophic lateral schlerosis (ALS)

LOU GEHRIG

that stole his strength and then took his life. ALS is still often called "Lou Gehrig's Disease."

{CENTER FIELDERS SUPREME} Near the end of Gehrig's

career, center fielder Joe DiMaggio arrived in New York. The quiet

DiMaggio led his teammates more by example than emotion. "He

did things so easily," commented Dickey, "people didn't realize how good he was." DiMaggio conducted himself with such grace on and

off the field that reporters began calling him the "Yankee Clipper"

after the elegant sailing ships.

With great defense and a .324 average, shortstop Phil Rizzuto won the **1950** AL MVP award.

During DiMaggio's 12-year career in New York, the Yankees won 11 pennants and 10 World Series championships. DiMaggio twice topped the AL in home runs, won two batting titles, and captured three

Most Valuable Player (MVP) awards—all impressive feats. But

what he accomplished in 1941 was truly remarkable. That season,

"Joltin' Joe" recorded at least one hit in 56 consecutive games, a

record no other player has come close to equaling.

As DiMaggio's career was coming to an end in 1951, a

20-year-old rookie from Oklahoma named Mickey Mantle arrived in

New York. Mantle was a switch-hitter who could belt mammoth

home runs from both sides of the plate. "There are some who say he

ROGER CLEMENS

hits with more power right-handed, and there's others who say

he hits with more power left-handed," noted Yankees manager

Casey Stengel. "They can't make up their minds. Now, wouldn't you

say that was amazing?"

Adding Mantle elevated the Yankees from great to dominant.

Along with pitcher Whitey Ford, catcher Yogi Berra, and shortstop

Phil Rizzuto—all future Hall-of-Famers—Mantle helped the Yankees win eight pennants and seven world championships during the 1950s.

Mantle's greatest season was 1956, when he won the AL Triple Crown, leading the league in home runs (52), RBI (130), and batting average (.353). He also earned the first of three AL MVP awards. Unfortunately, Mantle's career was hampered by injuries, particularly to his knees. No one knows what records he could have set if he had stayed healthy.

In 1961, for example, Mantle and fellow Yankees outfielder Roger Maris were both on pace to break Babe Ruth's record of 60 home runs in a season. Maris eventually broke the record with 61, while Mantle—despite spending part of the year in the hospital with a virus and then a hip infection—finished with 54 homers. "Nobody else would have played [with injuries like Mantle's].

Slugger Mickey Mantle slammed a major-league record 18 home runs in World Series games.

MICKEY MANTLE

Bernie Williams was the latest in a long line of great Yankees center fielders.

40

World Series. A year later, the Yanks returned to the World Series.

This time Jackson made sure they didn't lose. He pounded a record

five home runs, including three in the sixth and final game, to lead

New York back to the top of the baseball world. When the

hard-hitting outfielder powered the Yankees to another world

championship in 1978, Steinbrenner crowned him with the

nickname "Mr. October," since Jackson always seemed to play his best during the pressure-packed postseason games of October.

{MATTINGLY FINALLY MAKES IT} The Yankees reached the World Series again in 1981 but then fell to mediocrity for the rest of the decade. The Yankees' most consistent player during the '80s was first baseman Don Mattingly. The perennial All-Star won the AL batting title in 1984, was named AL MVP in 1985, and consistently earned Gold Glove awards as the league's top fielding first-sacker. He also inspired teammates with his burning intensity. "Check Donnie's eyes during a game," said New York pitcher Bob Tewksbury. "They're right out of a horror movie. He yells at opposing players. He paces in the dugout. I've never seen anyone compete with that kind of passion."

Although Mattingly was proud of his individual honors, he was

GOOSE GOSSAGE

Star first baseman Don Mattingly batted .311 or better for five straight seasons.

DON MATTINGLY

haunted by the fact that from 1982 to 1994, the Yankees did not

win a title. "For a lot of clubs, 13 years without being in the postseason

is no big deal," said Steinbrenner. "But for the New

York Yankees, it is unacceptable."

Determined to build another winner,

Steinbrenner took a good look at his team after the

1994 season. The roster featured Mattingly, All-Star

third baseman Wade Boggs, steady right fielder Paul O'Neill, and

budding superstar Bernie Williams in center field. To bolster the

club, Steinbrenner added free agent pitcher David Cone and rookie

left-hander Andy Pettitte.

The team finished second in the AL Eastern Division in 1995

and made the playoffs as the league's first-ever wild-card team.

Mattingly was in the playoffs at last! Unfortunately, the team's 1995

postseason stay was a short one, as New York fell in five close games

David Cone went 60–26 in the late **1990s** and threw a perfect game during the **1999** season.

DAVID CONE

to the Seattle Mariners. Still, the baseball world had been alerted:

the Yankees were back.

{ANOTHER DYNASTY BEGINS} In 1996, Steinbrenner hired

veteran skipper and native New Yorker Joe Torre as the Yankees'

new manager. Known for his calm demeanor, Torre quickly earned

the respect of his players. As one of his first moves, the manager inserted lanky rookie shortstop Derek Jeter into the starting lineup.

"The kid's ready," Torre declared. "It's time for him to earn his keep."

Jeter quickly proved that he was up to the task, hitting his first major-league homer on opening day and finishing the season with a .314 average and AL Rookie of the Year honors. More importantly, he helped carry the Yankees to their first AL pennant since 1981. Behind Jeter, Williams, O'Neill, new first baseman Tino Martinez, and ace reliever Mariano Rivera, the Yankees eliminated the Texas Rangers and Baltimore Orioles in the AL playoffs and then overcame a 2–0 deficit against the Atlanta Braves in the World Series to win their first world championship in 18 years.

The Yankees made the playoffs again the next year but were eliminated in the first round by the Cleveland Indians. That proved to be just a minor setback, however. The next three seasons, the

In **1997**, first baseman Tino Martinez powered the Yankees with 44 home runs and 141 RBI.

TINO MARTINEZ

Yankees dominated the league, reaching the playoffs three more times and capturing three straight World Series titles.

The slugging of Martinez and O'Neill, solid pitching by Pettitte and Roger Clemens, and amazing late-inning heroics of closer Mariano Rivera were all key features of the new Yankees dynasty. Yet Jeter truly sparked the team all three seasons, pounding

out more than 200 hits each campaign and steadily increasing his home run and RBI totals. During his first six seasons in the majors, the shortstop totaled more hits than any other major-league player had during the same period. And he was just as impressive in the postseason, setting a record with hits in 14 consecutive World Series contests. "The tougher the situation, the more fire he gets in his eyes," noted Torre.

New York struggled in 2001 but still reached the playoffs.

PAUL O'NEILL

Then, its October magic took effect. The Yankees battled past the

Oakland Athletics and Seattle Mariners to reach the Fall Classic for

the fourth consecutive year. After losing the first two

games of the World Series against the Arizona

Diamondbacks, the Yanks won three straight tight

contests, two of which they tied with dramatic home

runs in the bottom of the ninth and won in extra

innings. Needing just one more win to "four-peat" as world champs,   **29**

the Yankees finally faltered, losing game six and then giving up a

2–1 ninth-inning lead in game seven to lose the thrilling series.

    The Yankees express had finally been stopped, but the team

promised to be back. New York took a big step toward ensuring that

by bringing in free agent first baseman Jason Giambi after the

season. Yankees owner George Steinbrenner was thrilled to add

Giambi, a free-spirited slugger who won AL MVP honors in 2000,

Pitcher Andy Pettitte helped the Yankees win the **2000** world title over the crosstown Mets.

ANDY PETTITTE

Known for his classy style of play, Derek Jeter was a legend in the making.

DEREK JETER